My Sticker Paintings
UNICORNS

WINGED UNICORN (ALICORN)

INTERMEDIATE

RAINBOW UNICORN

HARD

FIRE UNICORN

INTERMEDIATE

PINK UNICORN

HARD

PRISMATIC UNICORN

INTERMEDIATE

ZEBRA UNICORN

EASY

ICE UNICORN

HARD

OCEAN UNICORN

EASY

FOREST UNICORN

INTERMEDIATE

BLACK UNICORN

EASY

ICE UNICORN

ICE UNICORN

HABITAT: Antarctica and Siberia

COAT: icy blue

MANE: golden bronze

HORN: solid emerald and jade

HOOVES: solid gold

DIET: lichen and moss

Myth and legend

Unicorns are very timid. Only young women with kind hearts can see them and touch them.

This unicorn lives in the coldest regions of the planet and moves around in herds. Its icy blue coat blends in beautifully with the snow, making it hard to spot. Its golden mane is encrusted with small emeralds and shards of jade. When it gallops, ice crystals take flight in its path.

PINK UNICORN

PINK UNICORN

HABITAT: deserts

COAT: light pink

MANE: deep pink

HORN: solid pink sapphire

HOOVES: solid gold

DIET: oasis flowers

Myth and legend

A unicorn horn is a lucky charm. Whoever finds one will be protected from illness and bad luck.

The pink unicorn's coat is dazzlingly bright, but it can go invisible if there is danger. Its horn falls off every 100 years and a new one immediately grows in its place.

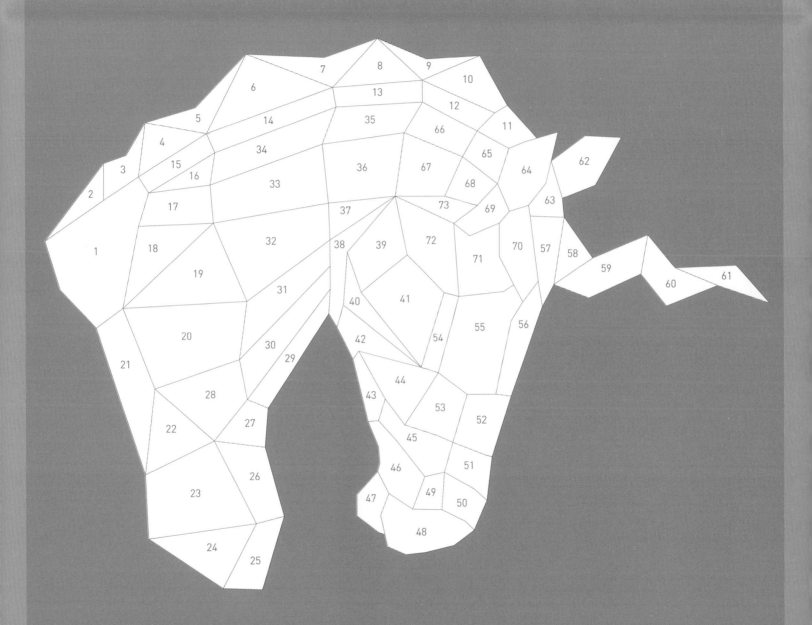

ZEBRA UNICORN

ZEBRA UNICORN

HABITAT: savannah

COAT: black and white stripes

MANE: black and white

HORN: twisted spiral, black and white

HOOVES: solid gold

DIET: dry herbs and thorny plants

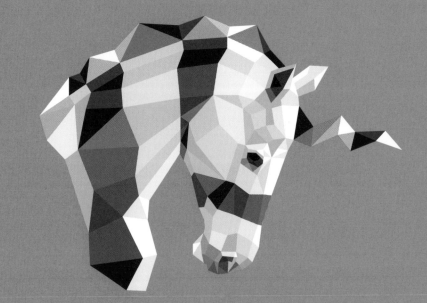

Myth and legend

Unicorns can live forever, but not if they are kept in captivity.

Zebra unicorns live in herds in the savannah. Their horns have the power to purify water, which is why other animals always let them drink at ponds and watering holes first. Normally skittish gazelles and antelopes feel safe in their presence.

FOREST UNICORN

FOREST UNICORN

HABITAT: dense forests

COAT: white

MANE: rainbow

HORN: solid gold, long and thin

HOOVES: solid gold

DIET: grass and leaves

Myth and legend

Forest unicorns communicate with elves and fairies because they can read minds!

These are the daintiest and most graceful of all the unicorns. Their coats are silvery white, their horns delicate, and their eyes azure blue. They live in the forest and protect its inhabitants from all enemies of nature.

FIRE UNICORN

FIRE UNICORN

KEY FEATURES

HABITAT: deep mountain forests and caves

COAT: orange-red

MANE: flaming

HORN: red

HOOVES: burning

DIET: ground insects and mushrooms

Myth and legend

This unicorn with a temper sets off forest fires whenever it's angry.

Like the black unicorn, this unicorn has a hot temper and lives alone. It is related to fire-breathing dragons of legend. It has the power to spit flames and start violent storms. Once per year, it travels to the center of the Earth to give birth to a baby fire unicorn.

PRISMATIC UNICORN

PRISMATIC UNICORN

KEY FEATURES

HABITAT: plains

COAT: multicolor

MANE: short and neat

HORN: multicolor twisted spiral

HOOVES: glowing yellow

DIET: grass

Myth and legend

Unicorns live forever because of the precious gems hidden within their horns.

This multicolor unicorn, the fastest of all the unicorns, likes to gallop across wide-open plains and grasslands. It can project a shining laser, brighter than the sun, that hypnotizes anyone who tries to capture it. The laser is so powerful that it can even pierce metal.

OCEAN UNICORN

OCEAN UNICORN

KEY FEATURES

HABITAT: oceans

COAT: blue scales

MANE: long and made of seaweed

HORN: solid ivory

HOOVES: two normal front hooves/legs and a fishtail

DIET: plankton

Myth and legend

Unicorns protect people who are honest and kind, but they refuse to help people who don't tell the truth.

The ocean unicorn is a distant cousin of the narwhal. It has the body and front legs of a unicorn but the tail of a mermaid. Its coat is covered in blue scales that shine underwater. It protects marine animals from the great monsters of the deepest, darkest seas.

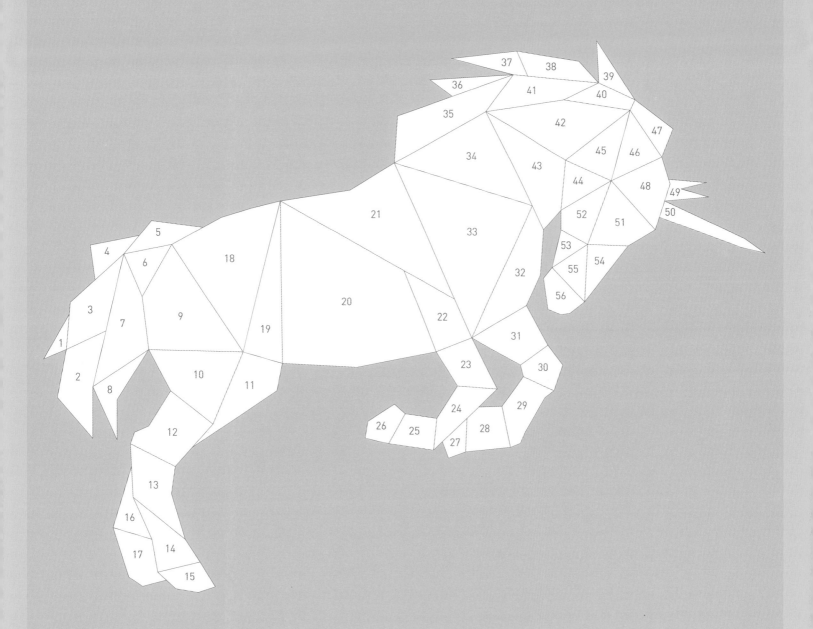

BLACK UNICORN

BLACK UNICORN

KEY FEATURES

HABITAT: large, old forests

COAT: black

MANE: black

HORN: solid ruby

HOOVES: red and burning

DIET: carnivorous

Myth and legend

All other animals are afraid of the black unicorn, except for the forest unicorn, which is the only creature who can challenge the black unicorn.

This wild unicorn only comes out on nights with no moon. With its hot temper and poisonous horn, it is the most aggressive of all the unicorns. Whenever it comes out, the forest around it goes quiet, animals hide, and even the wind doesn't dare to rustle the leaves.

RAINBOW UNICORN

RAINBOW UNICORN

HABITAT: sky

COAT: rainbow

MANE: golden

HORN: rainbow

HOOVES: rainbow

DIET: leaves from the tops of trees

Myth and legend

Whoever dreams of a unicorn will be able to see the future in rainbows.

This unicorn lives above the clouds and likes to dance in sunbeams. It creates rainbows and gives off a gentle glowing light. It has no need of wings; it simply closes its eyes and dreams its way high into the sky.

WINGED UNICORN (ALICORN)

KEY FEATURES

HABITAT: sky

COAT: pink

MANE: silvery

HORN: made of stardust

HOOVES: solid silver

DIET: plants and fruit

WINGED UNICORN
(ALICORN)

Myth and legend

Unicorns have a sixth sense that allows them to read people's minds and dreams.

The winged unicorn, sometimes called an alicorn, was the result of a love story between a unicorn and the winged horse Pegasus of Greek mythology. Only a young woman with a kind heart can ride it. This magnificent creature spends much of its time flying in the sky with the birds.

STICKERS

ICE UNICORN

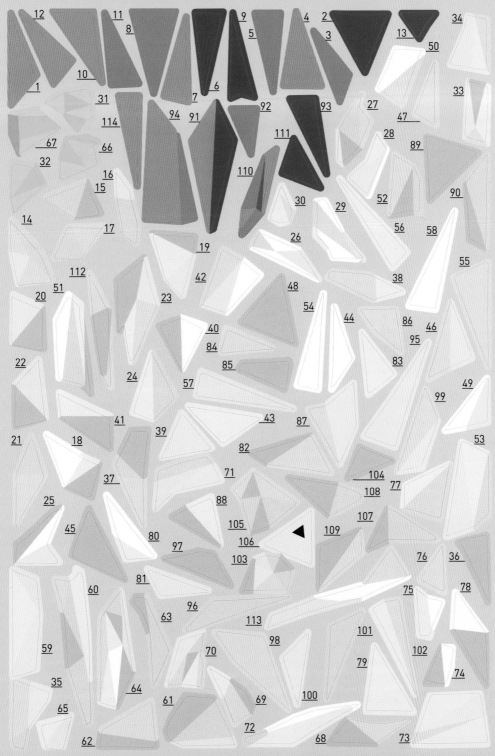

PINK UNICORN

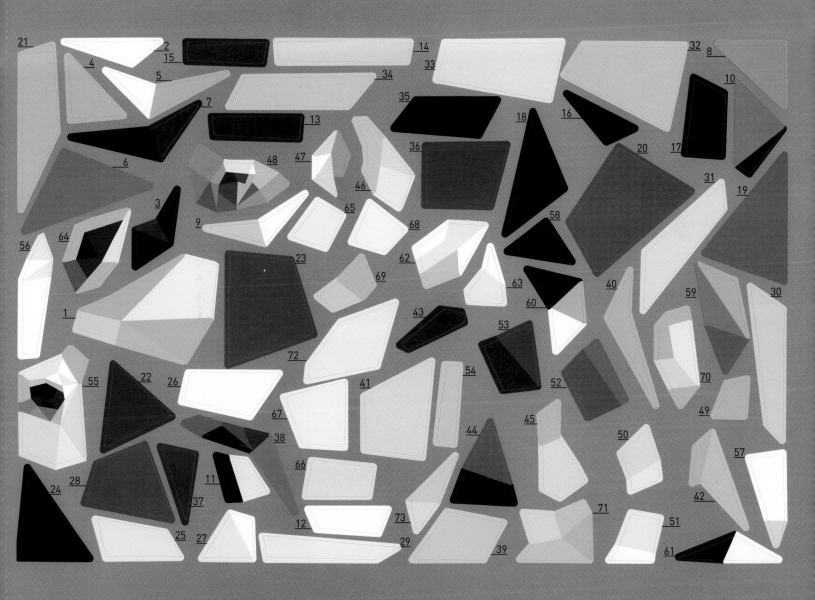

ZEBRA UNICORN

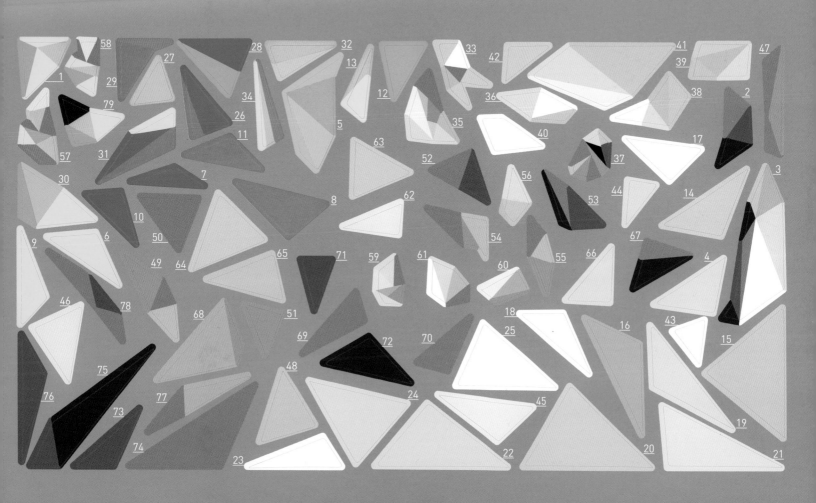

FOREST UNICORN

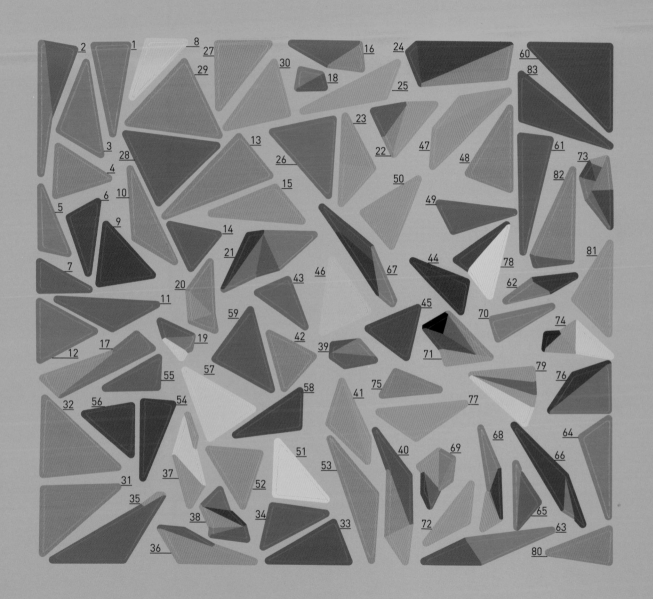

FIRE UNICORN

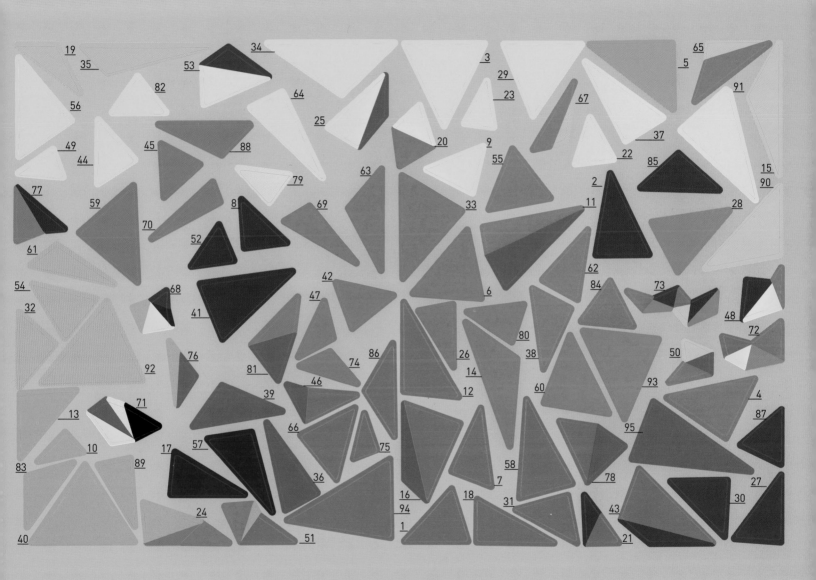

PRISMATIC UNICORN

OCEAN UNICORN

BLACK UNICORN

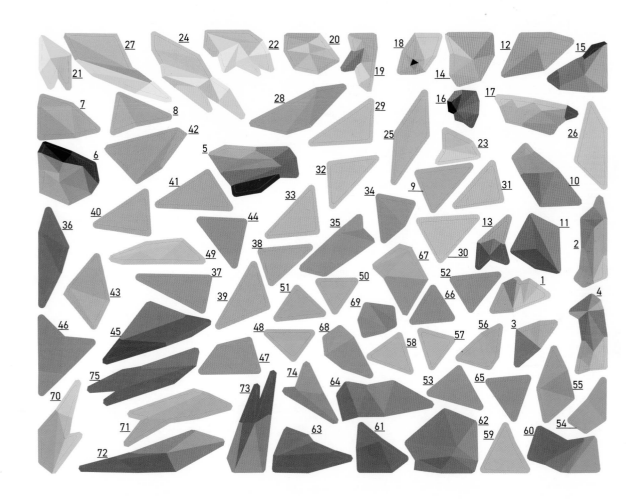

RAINBOW UNICORN

WINGED UNICORN
(ALICORN)